# Will We Still Be Here Tomorrow?

## poems on the way

Sunrise Press

copyright © 2024 Ford Turrell

will we still be here tomorrow? poems on the way

ISBN: 979-8-218-37329-0

all rights reserved. No part of this publication may be reproduced, distributed, or transmitted by any means without the prior written permission of the author except for those parts used as part of a review of this publication or its contents.

Printed in the United States of America.

For more information, or to book an event, contact:
sunrisepress3@gmail.com
@fordturrellpoems
https://fordturrellbooks.com

Cover illustration and design by Kurt Devlaeminck

For Kim, Amelia, and Evie

The path is clear from end to end—
    we emerge in just this moment,
from moment to moment,
                  —together.

## Starting Now

Starting now,
    you are living a new life.
It's not a life tied to the past.
It's not a life tied to the future.
It's not a life tied to a concept of self,
    or who you think you are.
It's not a life tied to a concept of other,
    or who you think they are.

## Baby Bluejay

On my evening walk, I came across a baby bluejay,
swept from its nest by the fresh Spring wind.
A few sparse downy feathers
barely covered its bumpy pink skin.
Its underdeveloped wings not yet ready to sustain flight.
The distressed parents called out, desperately
trying to drive me away—
but it wouldn't survive the night.
I wanted nothing more than to save its life—
I coaxed it into the long grass.
The other birds sang their joyful songs and looked for bugs,
apparently oblivious to the nearness of death—
Or maybe for them, death is the same thing as
stepping off the branch
and rising in the invisible current.

## Big Love

What if love is not a concept—
or an idea—
or a set of expectations to be met?

What if love is not conditional
or contingent—
or fenced-in by our fears?

What if love is not a label—
or a symbol—
or a brand to put on other people or things?

How much bigger could our love be then?
How much more could it embrace?

## Christmas 2_0_2_2

This year
    there are no Legos to assemble,
    no puzzles or games to figure out,
    no clanging tambourine for the family band.
This year
    a set of makeup brushes
    instead of paint brushes, markers, and crayons;
    cleansers, masks, and creams
    instead of capes, and masks, and dreams.

**Stardust**

Thank you God for helping me to know—

>my children's luminous stardust faces,
>the soft lump of their bodies under
>the covers after I tuck them in,
>the sound of their noisy chatter and tremendous
>laughter from the other room,
>the sweet smell of their skin and hair,
>their radiant warmth whenever they are close,
>the fine melody of their voices carrying "dada…"
>throughout the house.

If, someday, God
>my mind is no longer able to recall these wondrous treasures,
>or the people who embody them,
>or the memories filled with them,

Please, God!
Please, God!

>help my body to remember.
>help my soul to remember.
>help my heart to remember.

**When Lost…**

Start by helping someone.

## Resolutions

This year:

Listen more
Talk less
Smile more
Worry less
Pray more
Fear less
Love more
Anger less
Give more
Greed less
Allow more
Armor less
Wonder more
Know less
Create more
Destroy less

**Roadblock**

The only thing keeping you from being free—
    is a thought.
And you can let it go.

**Rainy Season**

In the middle of the night,
at the height of the rainy season,
an old teacher said to some gathered monks:
> "Everybody has her own radiant light. If she tries to see it,
> everything is darkness.
> What is everybody's radiant light?"

Imagine the rainy seasons of your own life—
> your own dark nights.

In those midnights,
> during the height of the rainy season,
>> where is your own radiant light?

Maybe you don't need to see to see it.
Instead, maybe you can hear it tapping
> a steady rhythm on your heart.

Maybe you can feel it in your longing, your despair.
Maybe you can touch it when you touch your fear,
> your pain, your grief.

Maybe its rich colors surface
> when you finally surrender and
> let your heart be broken wide open.

Right there in the darkest dark,
at the height of the rainy season—
Radiant Light.

## November Sabbath

The oatmeal burps on the stove.
The sparrows chatter in the hedge.
                The slanted autumn light
                              spills onto the floor.

## Guns (March 28, 2023)

Another school shooting.
Elementary.
3 dead kids.
3 dead teachers.
Shot—to death.
In the morning.
In a school.
By a gun.
By several guns.
By all the guns.
By everybody's guns.
By the gun of inaction.
By the gun of greed.
By the gun of fear.
By the gun of complacence.
By the gun of righteousness.
By the gun of history.
By the gun of ignorance.
By all the guns.
And I realized
That my tears are not my tears
They are the tears of a world
That just lost 6 beautiful beings
Of a world that has lost 1,300 perfect children
in the first 90 days of the year,
Killed by all the guns.

**Open Heart**

a broken heart
is an open heart—
an open heart
can connect with others.

**We All Fall Down, Hopefully**

True self exploration and
self discovery
does not result
in finding some
perfect multi-layered construction
of yourself; rather
it is discovering that
who you always thought
you were is just an accumulation
of entangled thoughts
heaped on top of one another;
And who you truly are
is what remains
after that artifice
collapses.

(This is not for the faint of heart)

## What If...

What if *you*
    released all the constriction,
        put down all the projects,
            and allowed everything to be just as it is?

What if *you*
    watched the steam swirling out of your coffee cup,
        listened intently to the silence of the
            house in the early morning,
                and sensed the lightness of the new snow barely
                resting on each blade of grass?

What if *you*
    noticed the self critical thought
        and let that thought pass by instead of
            judging yourself for having a self critical thought?

What if *you*
    listened to the clicking key strokes as your
        fingers navigate the keyboard,
            sensed the vast emptiness of the immense gray sky—
                like an ocean above you, and smelled the tropical
                    scent of grapefruit coming from a bag of
                      grapefruits on the kitchen table?

What if *you*
    let go of the struggle to control and manipulate

>   each moment of your life
>> in an attempt to stave off your anxiety?

What if *you*
> suddenly realized that this moment right now—
> reading these very words,
> sitting in the car in the pick up line at the school,
> saying "Hi" to the neighbor,
> opening up your laptop,
> is all there is in the entire universe,
> and that it can't be any other way—
> because this, right here, right now, is everything—-
> because anything that's not THIS right here
> is just a thought
> just an idea.

What if *you*
> suddenly realized that who you think *you* are is just one of those ideas?

**Rest Here**

Desperately trying,
    but what could you possibly lack?
When they get tired,
    the bumblebees sleep in the sunflowers.

**Armor**

He knows something now
about the urgency of time.
Death's hot breath in his ear.
His hugs a little tighter,
his goodbyes a little bigger
and brighter.
It wasn't always this way,
passing his time like he had an eternity of it.
Or maybe just passing it hoping it would pass
and he wouldn't have to feel some thing,
or so he could survive some thing—
some ancient pain maybe,
silently handed down through generations.
But he did the best he could,
and he's feeling something now.
I don't know what,
and he'd probably never say.
But I can see in him what maybe he sees in him—
the one thing that can't be denied or defied.
And it has opened a fissure in the heavy plates of armor,
and something is glinting through.

**Morning ~~Meditation~~ Commute**

Feel the relief
    of coming in from the rain,
        taking off your heavy overcoat,
            and entering the warm sanctuary.

**Blue Sky**

Three weeks of nothing but winter's
monochrome melancholy—and clouds.
With little indication there was even
a sun shining on the great earth, but for
a gradual lightening and darkening
during each brief day.
But today, today, today—
the clouds were gone,
departed for I don't know where.
But I felt glad they left.
And I realized that I had forgotten—

>　how vast the blue sky.

**Mad Dad**

Valentines Day.
Another school shooting.
3 dead. 7 critically wounded.
But probably not really big a deal because it was at a college,
and all the victims and wounded were almost adults.
Their blood, and cries, and screams for help are probably worth
a little less because of that.
And there have only been <u>68</u> mass shootings in
the United States so far in 2023.
Not too bad considering the year is only <u>45</u> days old.
At this rate, there will only be <u>543</u> mass shootings this year.
Probably not significant enough to concern ourselves with,
    or do anything about,
    or change any gun laws,
    or ban the kinds of guns that can kill 30 people with
    one pull of the trigger.

**Float**

It's ok
to stop struggling
and just float.
There's always
been something
supporting you.

# Mercy

feeding the dog in the morning
helping the kids brush their teeth
returning a friend's phone call
taking a walk and listening to the Adagietto of
Mahler's Fifth Symphony
making pancakes for Saturday breakfast
taking out the garbage
filling the kid's water bottles before school
telling a joke
giving someone a hug
accepting a hug
listening without a phone in your hand or on the table
making someone a peanut butter and jelly sandwich
cleaning the toilet
putting bird seed in the feeder (and spreading some
on the ground too)
walking in the woods and listening to the birds, and
branches, and earth
throwing a ball for the dog to fetch
folding the laundry
snuggling
sharing something about yourself that is difficult to share
saying a prayer for this one world
saying "I love you" out loud.

**Your Own Mind**

The thing you are relentlessly pushing against
        and that is wearing you out in the effort,

                is your own mind.

## Lab

Just as an experiment,
without worrying whether it would be permanent or not,
just for the sake of trying something different—
see what happens when you imagine yourself gently
setting down all of the baggage you've been carrying—
    the baggage of longing for things to be different,
    the baggage of fear of failure, and sickness, and death,
    the baggage of self analysis,
    the baggage of anger or resentment toward
        another person or group of people.
What if just for this moment,
you gently release all of those things?
In fact, what if just for this moment,
you also ever so gently release your sense of self—
of who you think you are or how others perceive you—
that narrow set of ideas that fences you in
from the rest of the world?
What if just for this moment,
you set those ideas down and you
weren't so separate?
How might that feel?

**The Boat**

Sometimes I row,
Sometimes she rows,
Sometimes we row together.
Sometimes we argue about who rows more—
Someday we'll realize there is no boat,

Then what?

**Just You Yourself**

Who do you encounter on the road?
No one but yourself,
> over and over again.

## As It Should

Can you sense how
this moment is somehow already
taken care of? Already
standing on its own?

The sap quietly rising in the trees to nourish
the unborn leaves;
the wind softly stirring the bony branches in
the empty grey sky;
the whole great earth rotating and
gliding effortlessly through vast space;
the moon, the tides, the seasons,
coming and going, appearing and receding;
these words materializing ~~on the page~~ in your mind.

Something is gently (and maybe sometimes not so gently)
urging us along—like the brown mallard
prodding her downy brood.
If we could just trust this urging. If we could sit back
into the energetic flow of it all, instead of always
being afraid of it, or trying to manipulate it,
then we might find that this life—
this one life—
is already unfolding just as it should. And
we participate in it by simply making space for its arrival—
and then allowing it to be.

**Ancestors**

You are your ancestors—
the farmers
the war veterans
the criminals
the teachers
the young widow
the racists
the immigrants
the drunks
the priests
the politicians
the abusers
But then, in you, your ancestors meet your other ancestors—
your 11th grade literature instructor
your church pastor
the lake
your favorite songwriter
your therapist
the woods
your best friend
your favorite poet
the stranger on the bus that you had a five minute
life-changing conversation with
the flowers in the garden

the 1,200 year-old monk—

And in this meeting of ancestors,

life itself changes,

something new is born—the cells, the strands,

the very nature of what you are evolves, resolves, heals.

**Great Black Lake**

On the great black lake,
> the geese honk, and splash, and rise in formation.

The low morning sun does not penetrate—
> reflecting sharply off the dark glass.

## What Is The Meaning of Life?

Cutting the last of the dahlia blooms before the killing frost.

**Rituals**

In a way, when you are in it,
you think you will be doing it forever,
running on the wheel of these morning rituals—
trying not to fall down the stairs in the dark
on the way to feed the dog,
grinding the coffee beans and putting the kettle on,
hearing the sound of the creaking wood floor as warm
bodies begin to stir,
listening to kids arguing over space in the bathroom,
seeing the sudden appearance of sleepy faces in the kitchen
looking for breakfast,
giving a polite wave to the neighbors when leaving the house,
driving the short distance to school (and thinking, "why aren't
they just riding their bikes?"),
smiling and saying "goodbye," and
"have a great day," and "I love you",
and hearing, "I love you too" as they easily drift
into the sea of winter coats and backpacks.

But sometimes, I cry in the car after I drop them off,
or when I'm at their music performances,
or while we're all sitting together at
the dinner table laughing and talking.
Because sometimes my whole body feels their absence even
when they are right there—

someday they'll move away,
follow their passions,
find love,
have their hearts broken wide open
by the beauty and the sorrow of this world,
discover who they truly are,
grow old (please God let them grow old),
get sick,
and die.

So sometimes
these rituals reveal themselves to be what they truly are—
pure unconditional love
crashing through the gates of my conditioning
and saying: "Look! Look! Here I am!
For this one, brief, flashing moment, this is everything!"
Can you see it?!

**Catching Up**
(as overheard)

We met at a coffee shop
and spent an hour catching up about
our amazing lives, our various
projects and successes.
Chat and smile. Chat and smile.
Sharing pictures on our phones of
our outward-facing, internet lifestyles—
at a concert, a dinner, a family reunion.
All's well. All's well.
But then, standing at the edge of my being,
I interrupted the simulation—and jumped.
I told you about my recent depression that
put me in the hospital,
the various meds my psychiatrist has me trying,
the days of sleeping 19 hours,
the 3 weeks of not eating,
all the thinking, and fretting,
the nausea. The fear of crowds and germs,
the unaffordable health insurance costs.
The uncertainty. The uncertainty.
And you, without hesitation, stepped into the gap,
and supported me in all the right ways,
in all the right places, at the very moment
I needed someone to catch me.

## Compassion

You're not the only one.

**Light Years**

Where does one person end and another begin?
Is there a way in which the boundary between you and other people is more fluid than you think?
This may be easiest to recognize with people you love—
> your children, or spouse, or parents and grandparents,
> a beloved friend.

But what about with strangers?
Or with people we hate?
There is no separation.
Where do they end and you begin?
There is no gap.
Einstein knew.

**Where is Mind?**

Walking across the ~~yard~~ mind
through mind
to get to the ~~tree~~ mind.

## Mushroom Clouds

We are still shrouded in the mushroom clouds erupting over
Hiroshima and Nagasaki—
still choking on the powdered earth and pulverized buildings—
still swimming in the souls of 225,001 beautiful people—
their fine residue soaking into our skin, seeping into our blood,
settling in our marrow.
We are still looking through the murky lens of reason and
calling it the blue sky—
still pledging faith to those amoebic plumes to justify
annihilating the "other".

I am the mushroom clouds erupting over
Hiroshima and Nagasaki—
June 1945—
Technical Sergeant Ford J. Turrell is chosen
to be in the first wave of United States Marines
to invade the main islands of Japan in an attack the Japanese
knew was coming.
It was going to be a bloody massacre on all sides—
the odds were that he would die.
But in August 1945—
some people in the United States with their own love-filled
families, intervened.
They discussed and decided that Little Boy and Fat Man
would incinerate 225,001 beautiful people also with families.

The war ended.
Grandpa lived.
He came home and had a son—my father.

I am the mushroom clouds erupting over
Hiroshima and Nagasaki—
Those great brown oaks
exhaling the oxygen that gives me life—
Atomic molecules that stream through my veins and
rest in my marrow.
My entire wonderful life, and the lives of my children,
grandchildren, and great-grandchildren,
rooted in a cataclysmic cosmic trade.

**Every Single Thing**

Every single thing
       is a full expression
of nothing at all.
And yet…
laughter in the kitchen,
blue hydrangeas in a white vase.

**NBD**

This fear of failure—
a bulging constrictor
slithering its way
through the dark passages of my mind;
its *raison d'etre,*
to slowly asphyxiate each moment of my life.

This fear of judgment—
a massive shark
emerging from the deep;
a shifting dark void
with arrow-head teeth,
ready to tear at the flesh of my freedom.

But then
I kindly turn to them,
carefully examine them, and
lovingly call them by name.
To let them know that I see them for what they are—
an oak branch fallen in a Summer storm,
a patch of seaweed drifting through the moonlit water—
just these ordinary beautiful things,
no big deal.

**Every Day is a Good Day**

So now you've seen the empty field—
the one in which wars are fought
and bombs are dropped
and we get cancer
and parents die
and children die
and we lose our memories forever
and species go extinct…
so what will you do now?

Be the field in which it all arises,
and weep
and pray
and witness
and help
and love.

**Menace**

The self is a sticky menace.

 

## The Jury's Out

Daily deliberation
on my own self worth
gets exhausting—
no one's waiting to hear the verdict.

## Sunrise II

Just a
sizzling spark
through the
silver-blue
cloud blanket,
yet,
bearing the power
to sustain
the entire earth.

**Walking the Edge**

How could you be more alive
than you are right now?
    It's simply not possible—
    no matter what your condition
    or state of mind.

## You Have No Flaws

What imperfections are there in nature?
If you really pay attention,
you may notice how perfectly it all moves.
But we generally think of ourselves
as somehow separate from that perfection—
> as though we couldn't possibly be part of the
> sublime movement of all natural things—
> as though we are not capable of it—
> or that we are superior to it.

But how could we not be part of it?
How could we not be part of that
perfectly choreographed movement?
How could we be in any way flawed?

**Bigger Boat**

Sometimes
    when you try to help others get to the other shore first,
God builds you a bigger boat.

## Oak Tree

I've seen you from every angle—
bathed in pink morning light,
trimmed with glimmering snow,
hidden in your green summer sheath,
dripping in the pouring rain—
but I still don't know you.

Your hulking roots
plunging into the dark earth.
Your colossal skeleton
reaching into the vast sky.

I wonder—
How deep do you go?
How far do you reach?
You answer: "Oak Tree"

Gazing at you from my car in the school pickup line
I suddenly realize—maybe it is actually you
who is gazing at me—
bathed in pink morning light,
springing from the dark earth,
reaching into the vast sky.

I wonder
How deep do I go?
How far do I reach?
You answer: "Oak Tree".

**The Open Door**

Death is a door that's always open
    and one day—
        you just ease through,
right into the birdsong,
the red maple,
the morning dew.

## You'll Never Get Your Shit Together

You'll never get your shit together—
nobody has their shit together.
In fact it's not possible to get your shit together.

This messy life,
changing from moment to moment,
from frustration, to anger, to sadness, to joy
is it.  <u>This</u> is how it works.
Not any other way.

If you can just realize this,
you can let go of the idea that there is something else,
that you should be someone else,
have things a certain way,
look a certain way,
be perceived a certain way.
It's never going to be that way.
It's impossible for it to be that way.  Because
that's not how life is.
Life just comes, right now, however it wants to.

## Remember the Winter?

Remember the Michigan winters
when it still snowed?
When the piles on the corner of the driveway
sloped over your head?
When the cold was so intense
your bones ached?
Now you don't even have to wear a knit hat
or mittens after Valentine's Day.
Now the unused dusty sleds just hang in the garage.
Now the summer birds don't migrate—
they stick around all year (but seem to enjoy it).
Now the lake doesn't freeze over.
Now the smallest creatures among us can't
hibernate under the blankets of snow and ice—
now there's no time for mother nature to gather her children.
Now the sap starts to flow and
new green shoots start to grow in February—
but then a merciless midnight frost descends in March
like an executioner and kills them all.
Now the harsh winter squall is nothing but
an early spring wind—and we comment about
how nice it is, and we go out and enjoy it,
and take walks, and ride our bikes.

But this placidity is only a disguise. It is just a
harbinger of something much darker,
something much more foreboding;
something we think doesn't affect us; something
we think will take a long time to arrive.
But it is already here—masking as an easy southern breeze
and as the Robin pulling worms in January, happy as a clam.

**Wind-Leaf**

When the leaf moves,
there is no wind or leaf—
there is only wind-leaf.
There is only [that sound].

# Will We Still Be Here Tomorrow?

## The Deep Clear Lake

First sip of coffee
    the deep clear lake
Crackling morning fire
    the deep clear lake
Every stainless snowflake
    the deep clear lake
The still mountain peak
    the deep clear lake
Baby's tiny hand
    the deep clear lake
Every single step
    the deep clear lake
The sound of every voice
    the deep clear lake

Death's sharp blade
    the deep clear lake
Never-ending tears
    the deep clear lake
Midnights in despair
    the deep clear lake
Every angry shout
    the deep clear lake
Silent pain screaming out
    the deep clear lake

Bright morning star
    the deep clear lake
Every breath you take
    the deep clear lake
This "word" on the page
    the deep clear lake
Every deep clear lake
    the deep clear lake
        with no b
                o
                t
                t
                o
                  m

**Water Flowing Into Water**

Can you hear the sound
of the distant waterfall?
of the waves crashing onto the shore then fizzing back again?
of the heavy rain on the roof cascading into a puddle?
That's you!
    Just water flowing into water—
ceaselessly.

**Til Your Ship Comes In**

While you were waiting
for your ship to come in,
for your dream (blank) to come along,
for more money,
for a bigger, better (blank),
for your pain to subside,
your depression to ebb,
your resentments to weaken,
and your karma to catch up:

> the dishes and laundry have piled up,
> the garden soil has been depleted,
> the dog has gotten old,
> your friends have moved away,
> your children have grown and left home,
> your eyes have drooped,
> your skin has wrinkled,
> your hair has greyed.

Yet, here you stand—
your hill to die on
nothing but a dream lurking elusively
beyond the horizon.
And while you've been lost in
watching for even the slightest flicker of motion,
your real life, this ordinary life filled with
ordinary moments of
joy, and sadness, and fear, and pain, and laughter, and love
has sailed right by.

## Death Weather

What will the weather be like on the day you die?

Brutally cold,
the whole world cast in an icy grey,
wind that penetrates the skin and slices the bones.
Visitors come and go, bundled in winter coats and hats.
Their bodies shudder off the chill as they enter the house,
and slowly warm while they parade through your room and take
their turn saying goodbye.

A rare spring blizzard—the unforeseen storm
birthed from towering dark clouds built by the wind over
thousands of miles,
slowly rolling over the great black lake,
letting loose mountains of white powder
that blankets and paralyzes every last thing.
Everyone stays home, wrapped in the vacuum of silence,
waiting for the message that you've passed.

The hottest day after two weeks of record heat.
Even walking from the house to the car is like
putting your face in an oven.
People drift from relief point to relief point—
the car, the grocery store, the bedroom fan.
Foreheads bead with sweat on the friends and relatives standing

near you while they discuss polar ice caps,
rising sea temperatures, and dying coral.

Cool autumn rain—
its soothing white noise through the open window.
The birds bathe cheerfully in the perfect, soft drops
and sing songs of relief—and wonder.
The chorus of sound drowns out muffled
conversations from the other room
about funeral music, Bible verses, and eulogies.

What will the weather be like on the day you die?
Will you care?

## Freedom Right Where You Are

Find a time to surrender every day.
Surrender to your fears and doubts,
your personal judgments,
your crazy thoughts.

Surrender is the beginning
of letting those things that we think hold us back
flow through us
so we, and they, can be totally free.
Surrender is where real freedom starts.

## Be-longing

What is this longing to be loved?
What is this longing to be someone special?
What is this longing to be constantly moving?
What is this longing to be somewhere that's not here?
What is this longing to be successful?
What is this longing to be famous?
What is this longing to be like someone else?
What is this longing to be free?
—When the truth is
There is no other being to long for.
> *This* is home—right where you are.
> *This* is love—just as you are.
> *This* is where you belong.

**Riverbank**

The crystal river
        continuously flows
                past the empty riverbank.

**Raynaud's Disease**

There's really no lesson to be learned from someone's death—
death itself is the lesson.
Its icy fingers constantly trolling over your warm body,
just looking for a way in—
"Knock, Knock".

## Constellations of Emptiness

The self—
a constellation of stars
in the dark night sky.
An array of shimmering singularities
representing who you think you are,
and who you imagine others think you are.

But if you just look a little deeper,
you may see that the velvety nest of darkness
holding those isolated sparks
is actually filled with endless other brilliances,
each of which could potentially be part your constellation—
if only you could allow yourself to see
> a little beyond who you normally take yourself to be—
> a little beyond your small, self-created zodiac.

And looking deeper still,
you may see that those infinite luminescent flecks—
> all those suns, and planets, and galaxies—
all those other universes
scattered across the vast darkness like confetti
are all arising out of . . . nothing.
That is to say,
all arising out of nothing but boundless possibility.
That is to say,

that you, right now, are arising out of that very same boundlessness,
and you always have been.

**Symphony of Tears**

Your tears in the car
are every symphony ever written or unwritten.

You yourself are the music.

Whether or not you choose to perform it in a certain way,
or at a certain time,
it is always playing.

**The Path**

The path is clear from end to end—
    we emerge in just this moment,
from moment to moment.

## Models

Holding onto a particular model
of who you think someone else is
or who you think they should be,
will only cause you to suffer.
There is nothing that does not change—
did you think they were the exception?

Holding onto a particular model
of who you think you are
and how you want others to perceive you,
will only cause you to suffer.
There is nothing that does not change—
did you think you were the exception?

**Torn Sail**

The mainsail has a tear near the foot.
A heavy headwind is distressingly
increasing the size of the hole.
Its gradual, contagion-like spread
can't be stopped.
The overtightened rigger
is putting grave pressure on
the cracked mast, and
at any moment it could drop
like a dead limb into the vast abyss.
The entire vessel is starting to list
from the accumulated years of
trinkets, treasures, and trash
stashed away far below deck—
a lifetime of collecting.

        Oh, what will become of us—
        adrift on this broken barge—
        this tired time carrier?
        We truly have no choice in the matter.
        The voyage ends when the blue sea
        and blue sky converge—
        and the horizon disappears.

**Tell the Truth**

Tell the truth.
Not being honest
in order to meet someone else's expectations
of you or the world
does not ultimately serve you, them, or the world.
It only creates
another layer of unreality
that has to be maintained and lived in.

**Offerings**

Do not believe
that you have nothing to offer.
You can always
offer your love and compassion—
especially to yourself.

## The Entire Universe

Help someone else
to see their blessedness.
By doing so,
you'll be showing them
the blessedness
of the entire universe.

**Already Free**

You are already free—
    You've just convinced yourself that you're not.

## Keep Pulling

This is the thread.
Keep pulling.
Til it wends its way,
    diagonally,
        back and then forth,
        in a half circle,
    over,
        across, and
            through
            the entire fabric—
until the fabric has completely
d i s - i n t e g r a t e d,
until it is once again just a single
t
h
r
e
a
d.

**Will We Still Be Here Tomorrow?
poems on the way**

**Ford Turrell**

copyright © 2024 Ford Turrell
will we still be here tomorrow? poems on the way
ISBN: 979-8-218-37329-0
all rights reserved.  No part of this publication may be
reproduced, distributed, or transmitted by any means
without the prior written permission of the author except
for those parts used as part of a review of this publication or its
contents.

Printed in the United States of America.

For more information, or to book an event, contact :
sunrisepress3@gmail.com
www.fordturrell.com
@fordturrellpoems

Cover illustration and design by Kurt Devlaeminck

**A Note About the Author**

Ford Turrell is a songwriter, artist, husband, father, lawyer, lake surfer, meditator living in Michigan. He has released three full-length albums of critically acclaimed music, the most recent of which features several members of his family, and has had several songs recorded by other artists and featured in popular television programs. You can find his music on Amazon, Spotify, Apple, and other digital platforms. This is his first book of poetry.

For more information, or to book an event, contact :
sunrisepress3@gmail.com
@fordturrellpoems
https://fordturrellbooks.com

Printed in Great Britain
by Amazon